# WELL

Getting REAL with physical and mental health

## CLARE DIMOND

Copyright © 2020 by Clare Dimond

All rights reserved.

No part of this book may be reproduced in any form or by any electronic or mechanical means, including information storage and retrieval systems, without written permission from the author, except for the use of brief quotations in a book review.

❀ Created with Vellum

*This book is for Bette who arrived in our lives as a wave of fresh air, fun, laughter and life.*
*Thirty five years and two grand children later, she's still energising us all.*
*(She is also very good at proof-reading).*
*Thank you for EVERYTHING Bette xx*

# Foreword

So many of us on the spiritual journey consider ourselves "seekers". We try and experiment with different paths, we meditate, do yoga, read self-help books, travel to India to do yoga teacher trainings or sit in a satsang. We might stretch it further and experiment with ayuahasca or other hallucinogenic drugs, or pushing our bodies into allegedly cleansing therapies.

The goal of most of the spiritual practices we undertake is to move us from where we are to where we want to be, usually to a happier and healthier version of ourselves.

In her exquisitely written book, Clare approaches this whole spiritual matter with the premise that, in fact "enlightenment is the realization of the fundamental perfection that the search for happiness is hiding". Her book requires slow savoring and the reader might want to go back to it a few times, as every time they will be surprised to find yet new insights and profound wisdom.

## Foreword

Clare reminds us that, despite the fact that we spend all our efforts looking outside for happiness, no book or course can deliver it. Her book points out that happiness and peace are already there, and that it is the belief in a separate concept of self that hides bliss away from our lives.

There is nothing to discover or fix, nothing to solve. However, when we hear that everything is perfect as it is, the mind feels lost, because our minds need to believe, need to think, need to plan. What is left when we stop doing? Clare's reply is: "Just this. As it is is. With nothing to change".

We have all experienced that perfection. It is that state we are in when we wake up in the morning, before the brain has switched on and thoughts and worries and plans have not yet gotten to us. We call it being "half asleep" and yet we are just happy, satisfied, and present.

It is that state of presence and bliss that we might feel at sunrise and sunset when we look at the immense changes of nature in those hours of the day. And yet we forget, or we are pushed out of it by the hustle and bustle of life. We try to come back to it through meditation, yoga, sex or by doing sports like surfing, rock climbing, dancing, that ask for a complete 100% focus. Or we slow ourselves down through shopping, alcohol, drugs, food, or scrolling on our phones. These activities give us relief from the pain of thinking, but they are a temporary panacea, not a definitive solution.

We come in and out of bliss and we seek to establish ourselves there. And yet, the seeking is the problem itself.

## Foreword

As Clare repeats: "the peace is here already, the activity of thinking obscures it".

Surprisingly, WELL does not shy away from touching controversial points. Clare points out the fallacy of non-dual thinking: spiritual bypassing. Just saying that something is perfect does not solve the tangible injustices of life.

So, how do we use this understanding practically? The answer comes at the end of the book, and it is further explored in the online course WELL. With her grace, wisdom and empathy Clare is certainly the living embodiment of that answer.

**Ameriga Giannone**
   **Founder of Bhakti Prema Yoga**
    www.bhaktipremayoga.com

# Contents

Part I
Introduction

1. A warning                                         3
2. A welcome                                         6
3. An invitation                                    10

Part II
WELL: concept or source?

4. Separation                                       15
5. Enlightenment - just another place to get to     19
6. Resistance                                       21
7. I don't get this                                 24

Part III
What are we?

8. The self                                         31
9. The body                                         34
10. Mind, thoughts and beliefs                      39
11. Feelings, state and experience                  42

Part IV
The real world of health

12. Escapism and transcendence                      47
13. Mind and mind management                        50
14. Beliefs                                         53
15. Therapy                                         56
16. Exercise and body work                          59
17. Diet                                            63
18. Medicine and drugs                              66
19. Diagnoses, labels and concepts                  70
20. Illness and acceptance                          74
21. Denial and intimacy                             78

| | |
|---|---|
| 22. Pain | 81 |
| 23. Death | 84 |
| 24. Healing | 87 |

Part V
Conclusion

| | |
|---|---|
| 25. Conclusion | 95 |
| About the Author | 99 |
| Also by Clare Dimond | 101 |

# PART I

# Introduction

*You are here.*
*However you imagine yourself to be, you are here. Imagine yourself as a body, you are here.*
*Imagine yourself as God, you are here.*
*Imagine yourself as worthless, superior, nothing at all, you are still here.*
*My suggestion is that you stop all imagining, here.*
**Gangaji**

# 1

## A warning

*The dilemma for the individual is not that the individual can't get what it wants — the dilemma is apparent individuality.*
**Tony Parsons**

This book must come with a warning.

It is a warning based on what people embarking on courses or conversations or books about the nature of the self can find themselves saying:

'I came here to feel better. But actually I feel worse: my sleep is terrible / my anxiety is increasing / I'm more depressed than ever / my physical complaint is intensifying / the suffering is worsening.'

And that, of course, looks like a failure of the course provider or author. The participant might even feel that they themselves are the failure. Because surely the only goal must be to feel better and to get rid of symptoms and negative emotions, states and experiences.

And this is where, right off the bat, we have to come

out with something that sounds absolutely ridiculous - particularly in a book about physical and mental health.

What if it was that - the identification with, personalisation of and resistance to certain emotions, symptoms, states and experiences - which is the only cause of suffering - and the only reason the suffering is prolonged?

And yes that sounds stupid doesn't it? Because it seems to fly in the face of humanity and reason.

And patronising. Like it's said by someone in some ivory tower of mental or physical health who doesn't understand how bad things are for us.

And dangerous. Because it sounds like it could lead to ignoring important signals or not getting treatment when required.

And confusing. Because why wouldn't we want to get rid of anything that causes us pain or discomfort? How can we possibly stop the resistance to it?

But how about, before we dismiss it out-right, we take just one moment to question what is going on here.

How could it be that a few spoken words, or a page in a book (or a facebook post, a google result or a headline for that matter) can intensify physical, mental or emotional symptoms and suffering?

What is causing that?

What is the link between some lines and dots on a page and the increasing of sensation?

What is the link?

This is the only question to ever ask.

If there is space to look at that, if there is a genuine readiness to explore what is going on there, then the portal to freedom (and to the understanding of true health) opens.

Without that space or readiness, the course is left, the conversation is closed down, the book is tossed away. And whatever is being protected by the turning away continues to be protected.

The link between trigger and suffering goes unexplored.

The causal relationship between what is believed and what is experienced stays unquestioned.

The physical, mental, emotional symptoms and sufferings will continue to change according to some hidden, uninvestigated factor.

Is it time for that factor to be looked at?

Is there readiness now to enquire…?

Let's see.

## 2

## A welcome

*When you're believing a thought or concept and you question it - you realise that it changes things. Every cell in your body is awake with enquiry.*
**Byron Katie**

Welcome to WELL.

Getting 'real' with mental and physical health is a very big subject.

It means exploring what is actually true in the concepts of who we are and in what is required for us to be secure, healthy and happy.

And this can be extremely confronting.

It confronts all assumptions and beliefs.

And in particular, it confronts three aspects of our identity that seem absolutely fundamental:

- I am this body, its appearance, its health, its symptoms.

- I am these thoughts and beliefs.
- I am these moods, these feelings, this state, this experience.

Three huge areas that apparently make up this self of ours and which tell the story, not just of our mental and physical health, but of our lives, of who we really are and of what we want to be.

Which is why the quest to feel better, secure or happy would logically and automatically lead to:

- trying to make the body more how it should be
- trying to make the thoughts and beliefs more positive and self-affirming,
- trying to make the feelings, state and experience more enjoyable.

That makes total sense.

But what we are going to explore in this book is that who we really are is…

- NOT the body
- NOT the thoughts and beliefs
- NOT the moods, feelings, state and experience.

We are going to explore how nothing will make the idea of self secure.

Nothing can do that, because the idea of self is only that - an idea, made of thought and belief. And believing that it is a fixed, objective, independent entity that is (or should be) in control of the body, thoughts, beliefs, moods, feelings, state and experience is the source of all suffering.

This is the fundamental misunderstanding: we are continually trying to make the self secure, not realising that the identity is a creation of thought and belief and cannot be secured.

And this continued, exhausting and unfulfillable quest to secure the self plays out in the attempt to 'fix' what the self is believed to be: the body, thoughts, moods, feelings, state and experience.

This can go on for a lifetime. The holy grail is to stabilise the self by securing each of these areas. And it will never be obtained.

Working on the appearance, health or symptoms of the body to try to make ourselves feel whatever it is we want to feel - worthy, lovable, successful? Or collapsing in self blame when yet another diet or exercise programme falls flat.

Trying to change the thoughts so that we believe better things about ourselves or others and all that happens is the negative self-talk gets louder, the beliefs of limitation and incapacity just get more believable.

Attempting to elevate moods or numb feelings or control experience to be OK and the numbing and control, while they may silence suffering temporarily, ultimately make everything worse.

Countless programmes, remedies, therapies, interventions and endeavours might be embarked on. Might even work for a while but then we will be back to the old suffering and the search for the next magical cure.

But in the exploration of what is real, that search must end.

The words: 'the self will never be secure' are the opposite of the outcome we are looking for. The outcome that we might have spent our entire life looking for.

So no wonder then, that symptoms ramp up when a course or book says categorically that the self identity cannot be secured, that the self is an illusion.

The symptoms - physical and mental - that are intrinsically tied into the quest to fix the self will go into overdrive. The quest is for security and control and when that quest is challenged, there is panic, confrontation, recoil. In other words, the symptoms that the self has been desperate to get rid of are very likely to get worse.

And because the unquestioned goal has, up until now, been to get rid of those symptoms then this is a disaster. We have to leave this conversation about reality and self. We have to avoid exploration and desperately continue the search for whatever it is will fix the self in place.

But if there is readiness, the search ends here in the realisation that what is being looked for can never be found.

And when the rising up of symptoms and sensations prompts curiosity instead of the need to immediately retreat back into the comfortable torture of the identity, then there is the possibility of something else.

There is the possibility of that search losing its life-and-death urgency and being seen for the beautiful, innocent misunderstanding it really is.

There is the possibility that all those symptoms and sensations tied into the attempt to secure the self, will find their home.

There is the possibility, finally of the realisation of the freedom and peace we really are.

3

## An invitation

*Someday, after mastering the winds, the waves, the tides and gravity, we shall harness the energies of love, and then, for a second time in the history of the world, man will have discovered fire.*
**Pierre Teilhard de Chardin**

This is an invitation to the absolute and infinite.

Maybe you are old enough to remember a time when television was something that began and ended.

Programmes stopped at midnight. And began again at 9am the next day. And sometimes there was no television in the afternoons. When there was no television, the screen displayed the test card or lines or static.

Not only was it tightly limited in time, television was of course also limited in scope.

In the UK, for example, until 1993, there were only three channels available.

And it could only be watched in the living room. Or in

the very posh houses on a portable tv on The Brand New Breakfast Bar.

So television was finite. Limited. What could be experienced and when it could be experienced was defined, set out, entirely predictable. There were edges to it - with nothing beyond those edges. No other possibility.

This was the reality of tv.

Now...

Trying to explain this to my kids who have only known tv as boundary-less, as unlimited possibility with no start or end, is... interesting.

They inhabit a paradigm of media infinity that just cannot exist alongside the concept of limits in which I was brought up. A boundary in time, geography, scope or space is, to them, literally inconceivable. (When it comes to tv viewing options that is, cleaning on the other hand has very strict limits that are apparently set in stone.)

But when we were there in the early 1980s, watching our limited programmes at limited times (while eating our crispy pancakes and wearing our fluorescent headbands), the infinite (much like good nutrition and subdued fashion back then) was unimaginable.

And yet it was there the whole time, just waiting to be realised. All that was needed for it to be discovered was the readiness for it. The infinite was latent, always present - just not grasped.

As it is for tv programming, so it is for everything. The limits are only ever false limits, believed and inhabited unquestioningly until all of a sudden they no longer exist and the unlimited is clearly all that has ever been.

Who we are is life itself - the infinite. We are not the tightly defined and boundaried idea of self. And the infinite is all there is.

We are the absolute and the infinite. Infinite love. Infinite peace. Infinite joy. Infinite possibility.

We might, for a while, celebrate the narrow wins of an extension of that limitation as we did the introduction of breakfast tv or the arrival of channel 4.

The equivalents for the self of that momentary extension would be, for example, satisfaction with the body, temporary peace of mind, a brief experience of what we want to happen.

But today, we are not interested in the narrow wins that just redefine apparent limits.

This is an invitation to the infinite.

To the unconditional.

To what has always been.

To anything else being inconceivable.

To who we really are.

# PART II

# WELL: concept or source?

*You are the awake space of awareness itself, within which all the "thought up" entities in your world appear. Out of all these imagined entities, you have simply made the mistake of thinking that one of them is you.*
**Enza Vita**

## 4

## Separation

*Realisation is not about you, the wave, realising it is ocean. The ocean realises itself in you and reveals itself to have never been just a wave. Nothing changes except the falling away of a false belief.*
**Enza Vita**

Imagine the ocean with a wave emerging from it.

Imagine this wave believing itself to be separate from the ocean.

Imagine this wave believing it needed to do something or change something about itself to be part of the ocean again.

Imagine this wave believing itself to be cut off from its source.

Imagine if this wave is us.

Imagine if every time we suffer, feel isolated, defeated, alone it is only because what we are has been forgotten, because an idea of separation has been believed.

What we will explore in this book is how, just as the wave is never, ever, ever separate from the ocean, neither are we.

Just as the wave is never actually separate from other waves, neither are we.

Just as the wave is never separate from the source from which it emerged, neither are we.

From the perspective of the individual looking out, the separation looks real. But separation is impossible.

Wave, other waves, ocean - all made of the same stuff. No divisions in any of it.

You, me, everyone else, source - all made of the same stuff. No divisions in any of it.

The wave is unique of course. It is a momentary, miraculous emergence in a subjective form.

The form of you is unique of course. It is a momentary miraculous emergence in a subjective form.

But the form is not separate, not isolated. The form does not exist outside of the whole.

And this means 'WELL' (the title of this book) could be understood in two different ways.

1. WELL as the concept of health. As part of an identity, an unquestioned commentary of how I am or other people are. A judgement of 'wellness' or 'illness' that seems to be fixed, true and which defines us or another as a separate being.

2. WELL as the source - the infinite, constant and absolute from which all apparent forms emerge and of which all apparent forms are made.

We are going to see through this book how the idea of ourselves as a separate entity is not reality. It only looks like it is.

We are going to see that this source or aliveness is the only reality. It just gets continually overlooked because it does not have the drama, tension and roller coaster ride of the search for individual security.

We will look at these concepts of separation and how they contain an essential untruth or misunderstanding that hides this source of unlimited, infinite potential that we always are.

The quote from Enza Vita at the start of the chapter sums it up beautifully. This is not about the enlightenment of the individual. It is about the realisation there is no individual.

It is not about me becoming more spiritual, more free or more peaceful. It is the realisation that the concept of 'me' is only a concept and it is that activity of mind and resistance that hides the ultimate freedom and peace of existence.

We will explore how this concept of self cannot be who we are. That it contains no fundamental truth.

The concept of myself as a separate individual is the epicentre of this storm of illusory separation.

As these concepts start falling away, who we are becomes more and more obvious. It will never be the case that I am realising this. It is the seeing that the only reality is the constant peace and freedom that the search to secure the individual is hiding.

So this book will be different in every way from the books that promise to make the individual secure, happy, fulfilled or peaceful. We will be exploring how it is the belief in the separate controlling individual that hides the security, happiness, fulfilment and peace that is already there.

This is the end of the search. It is the end of trying to make the individual ok. The search will never deliver what we hope it will.

It is the realisation of the fundamental perfection of life that the search is hiding.

## 5

## Enlightenment - just another place to get to

*The neurotic drive to find oneness simply falls away and then there's something that's very harmonious there, that was there anyway.*
**Tony Parsons**

We are exploring here how the belief in separation and the resistance to that separation creates physical tension and mental and emotional unrest. It is the resistance that holds in place these imaginary fixed worlds of self, other and reality.

In the absence of resistance, anything is possible.

And the mind or self would say 'Excellent. All I need to do is to get enlightened or be present or be in the moment and then all suffering will be gone. How awesome. Finally. There is a way to get rid of suffering. To at long last feel better'.

So we embark on a sincere quest to get rid of the ego. We read a ton of books and go on a load of courses.

We try to follow the right path and the right guru and the right action.

We try to become spiritual enough or evolved enough to attain that ultimate of all prizes - the end of suffering.

But here we are, still suffering.

All that has happened is that the quest for enlightenment has joined all the other quests in one big lump of dissatisfaction and belief that 'just one more' will be enough.

And this is because the search for enlightenment is just another activity of a mind that believes itself to be in control.

The quest to get rid of the ego is itself an activity of the ego. The more involved the quest, the greater the activity.

The individual cannot bring about the end of the idea of the individual.

The seeking cannot get rid of the seeking.

There is nothing to find, nothing to fix, nothing to solve.

And this, of course, is torture to the mind that believes everything is wrong. It is agony for the self seeking that eternal sunshine of the spotless mind.

But without that belief, or thought or seeking or resistance, what is there? Just this. As it is. With nothing to change.

# 6

## Resistance

*We think that we resist certain states because they are there, but actually they are there because we resist them.*
**Adyashanti**

Essentially, this book is a look at resistance to what is. It is saying that resistance to what is is the cause of all suffering.

This is a tough subject.

For many reasons.

Because it looks like we are saying the individual is responsible for resisting an experience and is therefore responsible for their own suffering.

Because it looks like we are saying we should be joyous —or at the very least neutral—in the face of even the most distressing of circumstances.

Because it looks like we are saying that action to heal an illness or to take away pain is resistance and therefore prolonging the suffering.

It is a very tough subject because we are not saying any of those things. But it looks like it because resistance can only be interpreted from the perspective of a controlling self.

But what we are saying is that there is no controlling self. There is no one responsible for resistance. It is just what appears. There is no one responsible for the actions to heal an illness or take away pain—they are just what make sense to do. There is no one experiencing anything. It is just what appears.

What we are saying is that the self idea and resistance are the same thing. The self idea does not control or manage or let go of resistance. It IS resistance.

That resistance, 'selfing' or activity of mind is the search for peace. It is the search for the potential, freedom and joy that we ultimately know is our birth right. But we are trying to find it where it cannot be found—by fixing in place the right emotions, or ending an illness or securing a guarantee that the body will never get injured or diseased and will never die.

We are trying to fix things in place that can never be fixed in place and when the body, mind, thoughts and experience don't meet the blueprint of how the self 'should' be then of course there is resistance.

So resistance is actually a powerful indicator.

It is a powerful indicator of fruitless activity, of an unfulfillable quest, of a futile protest against reality.

And we can see that it certainly doesn't help to add in resistance to the resistance…

When we hear that it is resistance that creates the suffering then we try not to resist. We get cross with ourselves for resisting. And so it goes on. In a never ending circle…

A vicious circle of self blame for something that the self is simply not in control of.

Let's say it again. The self IS resistance. That's where it

exists. It does not control it or manage it or let go of it. It IS it.

The falling away of resistance comes from the realisation that nothing can be pushed away and nothing can be brought in by the self. There is only what arises and the miracle intelligence of a body responding to whatever arises.

And what appears is that in that openness to it all, in the absence of any attempt to control, in the falling away, the suffering changes. The resistance was keeping it in place as a fixed thing. As resistance softens it becomes clear that there is an infinite intelligence at work, that the infinite intelligence is running the body, not only is there nothing for the self to do, there is actually no self in the first place.

## 7

## I don't get this

*When you understand something and live it without being stuck to the formulation, what you have understood dissolves in your openness. In this silence change takes place of its own accord, the problem is resolved and duality ends. You are left in your glory where no one has understood and nothing has been understood.*
**Jean Klein**

You might be reading this, if you have got this far, thinking what crazy world have I stumbled into? What insane nonsense is going on here?

If right now you are thinking I don't have the slightest clue what she is going on about, you are not alone.

And I'm going to suggest something that might not have been considered before in relation to the 'I don't get this'.

The suggestion is to notice that - in the moment of all that noise of 'I don't get this. I don't understand this.

Maybe I'm not the sort of person who will ever get this sort of thing' - that is where the self exists.

That is where the self exists.

In that moment, the self appears. That is where it lives. That's what gives it an existence, a form, a version. In that activity of 'there should be something different here'. And in all of that activity and busyness - what goes unnoticed is that underneath all that noise, all there is is peace.

The mind can only go so far with this but it is logical to notice that, if there were no thoughts, all that would be happening would be an apparent body sitting and or lying or standing, there would be apparent breathing, apparent reading or listening.

All we are saying in this book and in any other book in this series is that the simplicity of being is the truth. That is the fundamental 'is-ness'. That is the reality.

The busy mind creates these tremendous, compelling, all-singing all-dancing films of a ME and a BODY and HEALTH and HOW I AM and a PAST and a FUTURE and OTHER PEOPLE.

And that amazing kaleidoscope of activity has always been taken as reality. It might be that there has never been any hint otherwise.

And now that activity of thought is going a bit haywire trying to be peaceful, trying to find the truth in all the noise. But the activity only increases the activity. All it is doing is hiding the fundamental peace of being.

It is too simple to be noticed. The being-ness, the simple presence, this absolute 'I', this existence is just what is. All of the seeking is a momentary creation of a made up reality that hides the simple truth of being.

When, in reality, there is just what is.

So to sum up, when we are feeling that stress, tension,

isolation, wanting, needing, trying - that is a film of self going on. It looks real. But it is not.

And suffering is the sign of that confusion, of believing in a separate identity that doesn't exist outside of thought.

We have always taken suffering as a sign to go deeper into the film, to take that illusory reality as objective truth.

That is the fundamental misunderstanding at the heart of all conflict, exhaustion, stress and confusion. It is the belief that the suffering (caused by illusory separation) will be resolved by going deeper into that 'reality' of separation.

In this book, we are considering the total opposite.

We are saying that the suffering is because the idea of separation - a separate objective me in a separate objective world - is momentarily believed.

The suffering is exceptionally reliable information. The suffering is saying 'no answers in this'. When we wake up at 3am and thoughts are going crazy. There are no answers there. When we are trawling the internet, desperately googling symptoms to put the mind to rest, there are no answers there. How can there be? It is one insecurity after another. A rabbit warren of thought.

Everything we have been looking for is in the realisation of that. It has to be, because without that rabbit warren, there is just a body lying peacefully in bed. The peace is there already. The activity of thought obscures it.

But we don't realise this. We look in the rabbit warren for the peace and this only creates extension after extension to the warren.

The drama of the apparent reality obscures the fact that the space in which all this is happening - whatever word we want to use for it - consciousness, beingness, aliveness, unconditional love - that is what we are.

And we can go gently with this. There is nothing that

has to change in the suffering. That is the paradox. All suffering takes on a different hue with new understanding. It does not have to be different.

The thought 'I don't get this' is itself a miracle of creativity, imagination and love.

Nothing has to change.

# PART III

# What are we?

*What you take to be a "you" totally separate from the rest of life is really just awareness contracting or focusing on (i.e., identifying with) phenomena arising in awareness. The phenomena are the body, thoughts, beliefs, ideas, positions, opinions, emotions, sensations, experiences, states and all other temporary forms. As phenomena arise in awareness, there is identification. This identification creates a false centre known as "me."*

**Scott Kiloby**

# 8

## The self

*The self is no unmitigated blessing. It is single-handedly responsible for many, if not most of the problems that human beings face as individuals and as a species . . .*
**Mark Leary**

Perhaps for most of us, there has been the unquestioned idea that the self is an actuality. That it exists as a real thing or as an object.

We are going to explore in this book how it cannot be.

The self is not a thing.

It is an activity.

It is an activity of 'not this' - in other words it is a pushing away or an attempt to bring in or secure or a movement out of the pure presence of right now.

It is an activity of seeking. And this activity is hiding the very peace, freedom and happiness that is being sought.

There is a belief that the 'what is' is not enough or intolerable and that there should be something else.

And, of course, this activity of mind looks absolutely vital to survival.

When it comes to something like illness or disease, the idea of not seeking or not resisting looks like it will mean giving up all attempt to cure or treat. Because up until now, there has been no idea that anything happens other than through the seeking energy of the self.

So that seeking energy of mind says:

'I'm doing this. I'm in control. I'm making the appointments. I am saying the words to the consultant. I am taking medicine. I am finding out information.'

The self believes it is the one doing all that. So very naturally, in a conversation about there being no self, in comes the thought:

'Woah. Back off. I'm the one doing all this. Without me and my attention and actions, health can get worse, the body could die'.

This is very logical. But what we are exploring here is this:

It is not that there is a self that has no control over anything.

It is that there is no self.

It sounds so weird to say it but the self is not a decision maker or the doer. It is only an idea.

It is almost impossible to contemplate. It sound so absurd. But the billions of reactions and processes take place in this body without a self marshalling and controlling. Learning of how to shape words and move limbs was undertaken without anyone deciding to learn.

And it is the same with everything else, even the things it looks like we are making happen. Words said to a doctor are not said by the self. Words are just being said. And words heard are not heard because the self is making them be heard. They are just heard.

A glimpse of this is enormous. Because any shift in this understanding is a rucksack of weight lifted away. The self is not a thing doing anything. Belief says it is. But it is not.

'No self' is enormous and unfathomable but it is the only truth.

There are only two things to know:

1. There is no self in charge of anything, it just looks like there is.

2. Even if that idea of self disappeared, even when it does not exist as an idea - and this happens all the time of course - life continues to move the body, flourishing still happens.

The implications of this are stratospheric.

# 9

## The body

*To your brain, the world is just a stream of electrical pulses, like taps of Morse code. And out of this bare and neutral information it creates for you—quite literally creates—a vibrant, three-dimensional, sensually engaging universe.*
**Bill Bryson**

'I am this body'.

It looks so true doesn't it? It looks like the body is me and I am the body. There is no possibility otherwise.

It looks like there is an objective 'me' in this objective body, controlling it, that the 'me' is doing the reading now, that the 'me' is feeling the sensations, that the 'me' can use the body to be a better self, more loved, more respected, more successful.

It looks like the body is an objective truth. That the judgement on how it looks, feels and moves is factual and nothing to do with perception.

Which might be why this chapter might seem, at best, a bit ridiculous and, at worst, confrontational and offensive.

Because perhaps it is the hardest idea for the self to be confronted with.

Because the idea of a separate individual self arose through identification with the body.

We could consider it as beingness taking form within the body, lightly, as presence, spaciousness, awareness. But this taking of form gets mixed up in unquestioned identification with a controlling, deciding separate entity called 'me'.

Unquestioned.

But we are going to question it now.

We are going to look at how there is no individual perceiving self looking out through the eyes.

There is no individual controlling self moving the hands.

There is no individual self having these sensations and being the thing that is referenced when the body is believed to be healthy or ill, attractive or ugly.

There is no self that anything is happening to.

There is no self doing anything.

So what is happening?

We are considering here that listening is happening. Seeing is happening. Bodily sensations are happening. Perception is happening.

There is no individual self controlling any of this.

This is so enormous.

And it might, as we said at the start sound ridiculous or offensive.

But if we think about it for a moment…

How are you making reading happen?

How is conversation happening?

How is breathing happening?

How does a thought appear? How is it converted to a written word on the screen?

The mind (or self) has no idea.

It is happening as a series of intricately learned behavioural mechanics. A learning process that began long before any idea of self was present.

In fact, the self, itself, is a learned idea.

There is an apparent realism to the body and what it does, even though *how* it is perceived is always a function of thought and belief. There is a substance to it.

But the self… where is it?

The self idea is nothing but a series of beliefs. There is no realism, substance or centre to it.

This changes everything… and nothing.

It shifts understanding of what we are away from an idea of self as the controlling centre of everything. An idea in which everything is personal, every label, every criticism, every look in the mirror, every word and action is saying something about 'ME'.

We are considering now that none of it says anything about the self.

All behaviour is simply learned behaviour that will be carried out according to what makes most sense.

We are embarking on a journey which will reveal that the idea of self is composed of nothing but thought and belief.

And that what remains is simply the arising of sensations. Which can then be met with presence and realism. They are no longer met with the bewildering confusion of control, resistance and personalisation.

This is an honouring of the body as the pure intelligence of life itself. Its messages, its calibration, its alignment are met in a space that is absent of confusion. For the first time, perhaps since we were babies, the body starts to become known for what it really is.

The body and its sensations are what bring attention or focus as close as possible to reality. That is all we've got. What is being felt or seen right now.

And that is where intelligence is responding to intelligence. That is the place where everything is allowed and it can be met and responded to.

To try to fix or respond to or solve the flight of imagination which is anything removed from that visceral, immediate, supply of information is impossible. It cannot be met because it is not really there.

What is not really there includes all idea of what we are as an individual self. This is such an enormous, transformative shift of understanding.

Because the focus of our lives is almost entirely on the imagination, the personal, the projection, the idea of limitation. On everything believed to be real but which is really just flights of imagination.

The most real, most true information is that of the body. And that of course must be the healing space. We can't heal insecurity. Because we are trying to heal it by securing the self and that can't be done.

But this healing space of unconfused presence holds and honours everything that the body says. Trauma, past events that have caused real physical tension and contraction can all be held and allowed.

The more presence there is, the less confusion, the more the body reveals itself. The layers of tension and contraction are safe to give themselves up.

There is no resistance in that space. Without resistance there is just this visceral fluidity of information arising and being responded to. It is healing because it was the fixed idea of self, other, past and future that was holding in place the suffering. As the suffering of resistance dissipates, there is only reality, only the intelligence of now in full flow.

It is why this understanding of no individual controlling self is the starting point for healing. It is sane, real, immediate and intelligent. And from that space anything can happen. Conditioning can be undone. There is space for fresh new behaviours, actions, habits and practices that arise from the peace and freedom of the 'not personal'. It is a space of infinite possibility in which anything can happen.

That is the foundation of healing.

It is intelligence meeting itself.

From there, anything…

# 10

## Mind, thoughts and beliefs

*It is the process of thinking that creates the self, rather than there being a self having any independent existence separate from thought. The self is more like a verb than a noun. To take it a step further, the implication is that without thought, the self does not, in fact, exist.*
**Chris Niebauer**

We are looking now at identification with the mind.

It looks like I have a mind and that my mind is made up of my thoughts, my emotions, my responses, my associations, my memories, my experiences.

It looks like for the me, Clare, to be OK, the me Clare has to manage her mind.

I, Clare, have to control my thoughts.

I, Clare, have to change my beliefs so they reinforce my esteem or make me more confident.

I have to forget about such and such and remember x,y,z.

I have to make sure I find that right state of mind to be healthy and calm.

There is a constant reinforcement of that message over and over again. I, Clare, have to manage my mind, thoughts and beliefs to be OK.

So here we are this idea of Clare trying to manage this space called mind. And when we succeed in this then we'll be ok, then we'll have the eternal sunshine.

It is impossible to achieve.

Not least because that entire activity of mind in that moment contains the idea of self. That is where the self exists. As an activity of agency, of thought, of control. There I am. I wasn't there a moment ago. And now I've suddenly appeared.

I'm ill. I'm doing OK. I'm not exercising enough. I'm doing too much. I'm out of shape. I look great. I'm calm. I'm worried.

There I am. I exist in the arising of that activity. As a self, as an identity, I don't exist as that concept anywhere else. In other words, the self IS the mind. It is whatever form it takes in that moment. Then it turns into something else.

The whole thing is a spontaneous arising of thoughts, emotion, of other, of future of past.

It begins with the 'my'

My self.

My thoughts.

My feelings.

My depression.

My anxiety.

My hopes.

My beliefs.

My decisions.

My success.

# WELL

My failure.

They are taken to be two separate things.

Me and the thing that is mine.

But it is impossible that the self can exist as separate from any of this. It is one arising. There is no self having any separate form. It is one.

It makes sense therefore that any attempt by the self to control, manage, resist or change any of these things is only increasing the activity of that particular experience of self.

There's nothing wrong with that of course. There is no need for it to stop. It is just that no answers will be found there. Nothing that is being looked for will be found there because the set up is not true. It is based on misunderstanding and as the attempt to control and manage continues the misunderstanding only increases. No resolution can be found there.

And this realisation means it makes no sense to place attention on that activity. Like a storm or a whirlpool in a lake. It is just what is happening. It doesn't have to stop.

This is the realisation that there is ultimately no mind in the way it was believed to exist, as a part of my identity, as an element of who I am, as an indication of my stability, security, lack or wholeness.

This is extraordinary. Mind blowing - literally.

And it might sound crazy. But it is, ultimately, the only move towards truth, towards the ultimate health of sanity.

# 11

## Feelings, state and experience

*See, as best you can, that all sensations appear in your open, allowing presence.*
**Rupert Spira**

'I'm not OK.' 'This isn't OK.' 'I have to change.' 'This has to change.' 'I can't bear how I feel.' 'This experience is awful.'

Ever had any of those thoughts?

If so, you and me both, and perhaps seven billion others…

In the moment of that thought there is a deluge of evidence as to why that thought is justified.

And it seems very bleak and hopeless indeed. It seems this self has to somehow find the way to change itself or its state of mind or its experience or the world.

And that can't happen.

Because in the moment of that thought that is all there is. An idea of self and of reality created in that moment. And the thought 'this has to change' only makes that thought created reality seem all the more real.

## WELL

It's exhausting, this 'thought trying to change thought' business. There is no end to it. No solution. We can find temporary relief of course. Anything that silences thought momentarily will do - alcohol, drugs, shopping, work, food, exercise, cutting, gaming, sex, scrolling…

But that is only superficial. Nothing has actually changed in that. There has been no shift in the understanding of the nature of belief, of the transient thought-created self, of what is real and not real.

Suffering can be taken as proof that what is being thought or believed in that moment is reality and that it is without question, the 'reality' which is causing the misery. So to get rid of the suffering we must get rid of whatever is causing it.

This book suggests that that is a fundamental misunderstanding of the nature of suffering. And that this misunderstanding is the origin of all confusion and delusion.

Suffering, or in other words, resistance to what is, is the sign of confusion. It is the sign of something being believed that is not true. It is the sign that in that moment we appear to be something other than the life, awareness, peace, infinite possibility and love we really are.

To try to get rid of the suffering without understanding the cause of it (ie the confusion about who we are) is like sitting in a fire and taking pain killers to mask the pain. There will never be enough pain killers.

All of life is flow and movement. Except an idea that what is being experienced is somehow fixed and objective and must be resisted. That is a completely illusory position. At odds with its dynamic, energetic, vibrating source. It is stagnant. Unmoving. Unreal. No wonder it feels unnatural.

Resistance to what is would be like a flower curling in on itself because it should look different or a storm believing it was too angry or a summer sky hating itself for not being as exciting as the storm. That would be ridiculous, wouldn't it…?

Arrival, transformation and release. That's the design. There is the flow in - oxygen, water, food, ideas, thoughts, information, words, sights, sounds. And in the living, creative space of mind and body, they are uniquely transformed. An unmatchable convertor. The idea of self is just one of those creations, a form even more temporary and ephemeral than the exhale.

Health realisation, the end of suffering is the falling away of this apparent fixed self and the inevitable resistance to what is and, as this happens, the clearer and clearer unveiling of the flow of life that we really are.

12

Escapism and transcendence

*When you think about the billion-dollar industries that underpin the Altered States Economy, isn't this what they're built for? To shut off the self. To give us a few moments of relief from the voice in our heads.*
**Steven Kotler and Jamie Wheal**

In their book, Stealing Fire, Steven Kotler and Jamie Wheal calculated that the industry of 'shutting off the self' is worth $4 trillion a year. They included all the activities, substances, experiences and practices that ultimately have the result of shutting down - even if only momentarily - the burden of self focus.

As they pointed out, many of these are 'impulsive, destructive and unintentional'. They include activities such as legal and illegal drug taking, pornography and gambling that can of course, become addictions and create more problems for the 'self'.

The drive to turn off the suffering of the mind is enormous. And that is not surprising because it contains in it all the hardship and confusion of believing that the self is somehow separate from the world around it, that it somehow has to control itself and the world, that it is the thing responsible for behaviour.

None of this is true but the belief that it is can have the tightest grip and lead to an incredible burden.

And when that suffering goes unquestioned, when it just looks like the reality of ourselves and the world, we try to exit it, numb it, distract from it, silence it. Through whatever means are available to us. This is escapism.

Escapism can have the same result - the (momentary) ending of the eternal anguish - as transcendence or spiritual understanding - but with some key differences.

Without understanding, the peace looks to be the result of the drugs or sex or exercise or whatever behaviour led to the momentary peace. This sets up a continual quest with ever-decreasing returns. Understanding, on the other hand, is the realisation that who we are already IS that peace, it just is temporarily veiled by the activity of mind. This is not a problem. It's just the nature of being human, of having imagination and the ability to conceptualise.

Without understanding, the temporary nature of the peace looks to be something that has to be resisted or managed or compensated for. Dosages must be upped to avoid any return of the suffering. The means of escape must be on hand.

With understanding, it is realised that the peace we really are is often hidden when the activity of mind ramps up.

And that this happens when beliefs that are core to the identity are protected. 'Ramping up' is understood for what it is—the conditioned separation of the self being made transparent, available for understanding and acceptance.

The activity of the mind therefore, far from being something that must be escaped, is revelatory and an 'undoing of self'.

This torment, this suffering of separation can actually become, believe it or not, something to look forward to.

# 13

## Mind and mind management

*The separate self (mind) is not an entity. It is an activity: the activity of resisting what is present and seeking what is not present.*
**Rupert Spira**

Without an understanding of what the mind really is, mind management is just a playing out of confusion.

The self exists as a thought or belief or as a state of mind. It arises in that moment in whatever appearance it takes on. It doesn't exist outside of that. The idea of who we are is whatever the mind is doing in that moment.

For the self to try to manage the mind creates a false separation and unfulfillable effort. Because self and mind are the same thing. A belief trying to manage other beliefs creates a circular confusion that goes nowhere.

We can see this in techniques like meditation and mindfulness which can be extraordinarily powerful when they are understood for what they are and frustrating and hopeless when they are not.

Meditation is the making transparent of all thought. It is the witnessing of whatever activity of mind there is.

It is a spotlight placed on the *whole activity of mind* - which has to include all idea of self.

All of it - including the idea of self - is seen for the transient procession it is. The way the self appears in thought is no different from any other thought. And so the whole idea of reality, the whole idea of circumstance, events and concepts AND the whole idea of self are seen for what they are: thought.

But when the self and mind are not understood and meditation is believed to be a way that the self can control thought or clear the mind or make the self peaceful, then an inner battle is set up that only creates more unrest.

The self is judging itself. The self is trying to control itself. Yet it is that very activity of attempting to manage all this that IS the activity of mind. The attempt to manage IS the busyness.

When it looks like the self is separate from the thoughts and beliefs then there is confusion. When it is understood that everything is made of thought then the whole activity of mind is seen for what it is.

It is the same with mindfulness. When we are striving to be mindful, then the very opposite of what mindfulness sets out to achieve is happening.

Mindfulness is the space of presence in which whatever arises is fully experienced or felt. Mindfulness is a description of what we really are. That is what we are. That space.

And the idea of self is only an activity that obscures that absolute space and presence. The idea of self makes us out to be a limited separate being. And this is hiding the infinite space of completeness that we really are.

Mind techniques, with the understanding that the

activity of mind is the self, are extraordinarily powerful pointers to what is true.

Without it, they are just additional confusion and seeking activity that further hides our true nature.

## 14

## Beliefs

*I can negate my beliefs because my beliefs change all the time. They are not real, they are not me either. But the one who knows — the awareness or the consciousness that knows — is eternal. Try to negate yourself, try to remove yourself from this equation. You can't do it.*
**James Swartz**

There are many techniques that seek to change the patterns of thought, belief and association, that aim to change the fundamental set up of how responses are structured. For example Cognitive Behavioural Therapy, or Neuro-linguistic programming or hypnosis.

That aim to create a healthier, or more peaceful or more considered response.

I've done an awful lot of this to advance and mastery levels and have seen some enormous transformation. Phobias can be dissolved. Old patterns can change completely.

But when we try to change beliefs, we are trying to do

that from within a belief system. What says whether a belief is good or bad, helpful or unhelpful, healthy or toxic? Only another belief.

Trying to change what is believed will always come from a conditioned idea of the right thing, of the right way to behave, which is ultimately a cultural or societal idea. Which of course comes from the idea of what would create an easier life, what would create a fit within these social customs.

But if we really want to give the mind and body their full space and potential, instead of manipulating the mind to change from one belief to another, from one idea of self to another, it is so much saner, more real, less confused to consider that no belief is ever true, that no belief is ever the right one, that no thought is ever anything other than a transient experience passing through.

And that is why people who are seeking the truth about themselves and the world will continue moving through these different cognitive interventions until the entire nature of belief, thought and self is seen for what it is. Without that, there is a sense of restriction and 'unreality', a sense of blindly moving furniture around without understanding the nature of the building itself.

Even if my public speaking phobia had been cured by hypnosis or NLP (which it never was incidentally) then there would be another thing, then another. As long as the self idea remains unquestioned and as long as that very idea of self is an activity of identifying these things that have to be conquered then there is always going to be this restless unease and on-going seeking.

This is where it gets super interesting because it is through that realisation that techniques like CBT, NLP and hypnosis THEN come into their own. Because then they are only about the reality of this body mind entity. They are not about taking on the impossible task of trying to fix the self identity. They are not saying 'this reality is real'. They are simply practical ways of addressing quirks of thought.

Then everything falls away and there is no longer that grip of identification. And then there is this immersion of life in form. There might still be a fear of snakes or a smoking habit or a tendency towards anger or there might not be and, whether there or not, these things say nothing about the self. There is nothing personal in them. They are tendencies learned in the development and conditioning of the body-mind. And it might make sense for them to be addressed.

These techniques then just become very practical ways to alter a quirk of the mind and body. And nothing beyond that.

Just in the way that we might eat a meal when we are hungry or go for a walk. It doesn't have the weight of expectation of fixing the self. It is just the practical response to the on-going needs of the body or mind.

Nothing is ruled out in this understanding. in fact everything comes in as options. But options within sanity. Not the misunderstanding of 'oh my god will this finally make ME OK?'

It couldn't be more different.

## 15

## Therapy

*In truth, there is no patient, no 'other' person to heal. But this, ironically, brings about excellent results, because 'I' have gotten out of the way, so Love can flow unobstructed.*
**Mandi Solk**

Therapy is an interesting intervention to consider in the light of who we really are.

At one level, we could say the mind is only an activity of self and so there is never any need for therapy. But that would really be a spiritual bypassing of the psychological suffering that so many of us endure.

And it doesn't acknowledge the very many people who have been helped by great therapy or by a great therapist who has helped the mind to settle or the client to see another perspective.

When the therapist has a good understanding of the shifting nature of the past, the thought created idea of self and of reality, when the therapist has seen this for themselves, in their own life then therapy or counselling can be transformational.

So instead of investigating the past as a fixed, objective truth that the client has to come to terms with, there would be an understanding that the past is fluid, that the whole way it appears is wholly dependent on what is understood about self and other.

Approaching a healing conversation from that space, is not only true, practical and realistic, it is a space of potential. It is a space in which the true flow of life and intelligence can be revealed.

Without that, then all the therapy is doing is cementing in place a belief or concept as actually reality, and the more we explore, the deeper into the story we go. So it would have the opposite of the intended effect. Which would be why, instead of being set free in the shortest possible time, a patient can end up in the same therapeutic relationship, utterly dependent, for decades.

Which brings us to the other consideration of the dynamic between therapist and client. And the therapist's own understanding of what they are and of how the client is only ever a mirror of that.

Without an understanding of the nature of self and reality, the therapist is viewing the client through unquestioned belief, bias, association and limitation. The client appears through that perspective and that will dictate the dynamic of that session. All conversation will happen within that limited frame of what the therapist believes. In a way there is no actual reality going on for the therapist, they are just speaking into a mirror of themselves.

But when the therapist has gone so deeply into their own work, so deeply into the understanding of self and other, when there is a profound understanding that no belief can ever be true and yet a belief will dictate the whole experience of reality, then there is no therapist in the room, there is just the open space of presence, potential and love.

In other words, when the therapist IS the open space of unconditional love, that knowing of potential will talk directly to that in the client. The whole dynamic is one of possibility. It isn't hemmed in by what I the therapist believe about you the client (which is really only what I believe about me).

Within that fresh open dynamic that is nothing but potential and presence, enormous change can take place for both client and therapist. Everything can be explored in that space - the deepest trauma, the biggest fears, the most destructive habits and behaviours - it can all be voiced and investigated from an understanding of reality. This is the ultimate honouring space.

Which is why, for many of us, after trying every sort of therapy and intervention, we land in a conversation about reality and for the first time something profound shifts. And then, for the first time, therapy can have real value and impact.

Until there is a realisation of the transient, created nature of the self identity, all we are doing is carting this self around the various practices, asking them to fix in place and secure that which can never be secured.

# 16

## Exercise and body work

*The hardest thing to hear is that the body doesn't need us. It doesn't need our seeking, it doesn't need our suffering, it doesn't need our identity. It functions effortlessly without us.*
**Jeff Foster**

In this chapter we will look at the dynamic between body, thoughts, beliefs and the idea of self, and the implications that has for exercise, fitness, movement and sport.

We're told or conditioned to believe that if we can get the body into peak fitness then everything will be ok. There is an ideal of how healthy we can be physically which will then sort out our worries and concerns and will lead to much more peace of being.

This is interesting because it is certainly often the case that a form of clearing can happen with exercise. There can be a zone or a flow in which any idea of who we are falls away, stress falls away. There is just presence in the form of a body and there is a sense of peace and wholeness in the midst of the run or class or wherever we are.

And there is much evidence of the psychological and cognitive benefits of exercise - improving memory and sleep, alleviating mood and anxiety, reducing stress.

And this is where it can get confusing because it can look like the exercise is helping *me* but, in reality the increased oxygen, movement and distraction is simply allowing the tightness of thoughts of what I am and what I have to do to dissipate. The exercise reveals what was already there, underneath, which was hidden by the activity of mind.

But where we go wrong with this is that the zone or flow or peace that is experienced looks like it is something outside of us or a destination that was achieved through the exercise. It looks like it is somehow separate from me, that the exercise created the state.

But as we start looking more closely at what the self is everything starts to shift. What we start to see is that we already are the flow of life itself. We are the zone. We are the completeness and wholeness. We are that already. It's just that, ironically, it gets hidden by the search for it.

And believing that exercise brings it in, as opposed to reveals it, sets up a search or a seeking to attain that state. Much like a win for an athlete, that relief of winning can become the destination, the driving force. Everything is done to create that thing that has to be found and brought in. Exercise, in this confusion, is no different to a bottle of whisky.

I remember talking to a young woman a while ago. Running had become a critical part of her life. If she didn't run then nothing felt right. Then one day when she was out pounding the pavement she had a sudden realisation that literally stopped her in her tracks. It hit her that there will never be enough running for her to be ok. The training shoes, the pavement and the legs would run out long before the search for guaranteed peace would.

This recognition of the never-ending seeking of the mind transformed exercise for her. Running stopped being about the search and instead became a space of playfulness. The simple expression of aliveness without the weight of a self to secure.

We can see how the drive to find ourselves, to secure a state of mind through the exercise, sport or the perfect body shape can be a phenomenal drive. It can be a drive so powerful that, in its relentless dissatisfaction, it ultimately destroys the body.

It is a drive that comes from misunderstanding.

Ultimately there will never be enough victories or miles under the belt or enough muscles or enough tone or enough physical improvements to satisfy that ultimate unfulfillable quest of trying to be what we think we should be.

You might have seen the episode of Louis Theroux talking to people who have extreme, almost continuous plastic surgery. There will never be enough operations to fix the belief in an insecure self. Anything can become a bottomless pit when we believe that is where our happiness and fulfilment will be found.

But with realisation of what we are, the behaviours of the body align to completeness, to security. And all behaviour, instead of charting the search for security instead becomes the simple expression of life.

The whole set up becomes one of sanity and peacefulness in which the body takes its rightful place.

It is always the case - understand the nature of the self first, before anything else.

Understand the nature of reality.

Understand where insecurity arises from.

Then everything else takes care of itself.

Including, perhaps especially, something as fundamental as the movement of the body.

# 17

## Diet

*If you live and then die convinced you're the one you see in the mirror, you've missed out on what is your birthright, which is awakening to who you really are.*
**Richard Lang**

Let's look now at diet and health.

We were talking in a small group recently about binge eating. One of the participants told us their eating pattern was totally out of sync with what they want it to be. They were eating junk food every evening and then were full of self blame which then led to more feelings of hopelessness and more binge eating.

What to do about that?

It can look like the way to make the self stable or stop the neediness is through more control of what we're eating. It can look like the way out is more will power, more discipline, more self. Which is why, when we are sitting there in front of the tv eating the stuff we have promised ourselves we wouldn't, we can feel so hopeless and full of self hatred. The constant play of the mind 'Eat it. Eat it. Eat it' flipping to 'Why did you eat it? You shouldn't have eaten it'.

But equally, we can see how control can easily flip to the other side, for example, the hyper-vigilance that an anorexic person exerts over their diet in an attempt to bring about a sense of stability.

But no-control and control are both only coming from the same conditioned thinking that created this whole confusion in the first place.

All behaviour - even that which seems very damaging to health is absolutely logical given what is being believed. In fact it is futile to try to change the behaviours because they are the perfect behaviours given what is being understood.

Peace won't be found in food or in control.

Instead, what we can see is that the focus on behaviour and wrong and right, the actions and then the judgement all create an intense busyness of mind. An intensity of 'selfing' as Paul Hedderman, a teacher in this understanding, might describe it.

As anyone who has tried and failed to manage their behaviour will know, this 'selfing' is a vicious circle. It is impossible to separate out mind, body and self - it is one system. A vicious circle increasingly out of sync with reality and its natural space of flourishing. Which in turn leads to more self insecurity and to more and more extreme behaviours to try to fix that discomfort. There is no solution here.

The only portal out of this confusion is the deep enquiry into who or what we are.

That enquiry will lead to the realisation that there is no possibility of securing this idea of self. It cannot be secured. It is made of thought.

So all attempt to secure it through diet is absolutely futile. And that starts to shift the understanding of reality. It becomes clear that what is real is this. Just this. What is happening now. Everything else is just imagination. There is increasing response to now. And that is the space in which the body can flourish. It is the space in which the mind can settle because it is not chasing off trying to solve problems of imagination. It is meeting what is real.

Behaviours such as eating are no longer seen as a solution to the insecure self or as evidence of a good or a bad self or as reward or punishment, distraction or numbing. And instead become just the natural response to the reality of the body.

There is more integration, more alignment.

The body is allowed to exist in and respond to reality.

That is the design of us. That is the sanity of health that is our birth-right.

## 18

## Medicine and drugs

*The clear mind understands that the body is not personal. It can't cause any problems; mind's identification with the body is what causes the confusion and suffering.*
**Byron Katie**

The big question when it comes to medicine and drugs is: what are they trying to fix?

Which leads us to the question: what is giving rise to the symptoms and the suffering?

There is no denial of illness and the effectiveness of treatment here. My sister was born with Cystic Fibrosis, and had a heart and lung transplant. My father died age 43 of leukaemia. Of course there are physical issues in the body and brain and there is medicine that will be able to cure them or at least alleviate them.

There is nothing more obnoxious than someone under the guise of 'spirituality', but really pure egoic superiority, trying to make out that physical issues are all in the mind and if only that misguided soul meditated or chanted then they would be healed.

A salutary lesson on this for me was at university when one of our friends had terrible stomach pains on the day of graduation. 'It's the stress' every one said with wise expressions on their faces. 'It's the tension from the exams coming to a head."

A collapse, an ambulance and emergency surgery confirmed the acute appendicitis that, had it not been acted on just in the nick of time, would have killed her.

Using the understanding of true nature to deny the body, illness or treatment is a nonsense.

What is fascinating, though, is how the understanding of no self to secure removes the confusion about what illness is and what medicine can achieve.

Now the mind can't do this. Because the mind is where the self and reality exist, then the mind will always believe the version of self and reality it creates. It is never any use asking the mind what is causing anything related to the personal because all that will come out is the personal story.

That personal story is aways some form of resistance to whatever is happening now. Resistance only lessens as the idea of a controlling self becomes less believable and the desire to secure an insecure self that is made of thought becomes more ridiculous.

Ironically it is the lessening of resistance to the illness or pain that allows the illness or pain to be seen more clearly and therefore treated more appropriately. Until then, treatment doesn't have to just treat the issue it has to somehow also treat the belief that the issues shouldn't be there. Drugs can do that of course, take away the mental pain, bring about a numbness that removes the pain of imagined separation. But it is no solution. And that addiction to the medication that solves the fundamental anguish of believing ourselves to be a separate individual is no joke.

The end of the confusion lies in the purely physical. It lies in the dissolution of the idea that whatever is happening shouldn't be happening, that whatever is happening is personal in some way.

A good analogy would be me turning up to a garage with my car in tow expecting the mechanics to not just fix the car but also my frustration at the car breaking down and the suffering caused by the idea that the issues with the car are happening to me.

Medicine cannot solve the unease of imagined separation. Only realisation can do that. Drugs can temporarily numb it but, as we all know, without understanding, they will just increase the suffering of separation.

All we can do is take whatever medicine makes sense for us in this moment. Whatever it is - take that.

AND at the same time, let's consider what is true, where confusion lies, where there is an attempt to fix something that can never be secured and where drugs are seen as a viable way to secure that thing that can never be secured.

While there is confusion about who we are, there will be confusion about what the drugs and treatment can do. Just as there is confusion about everything. That's ok. We will just take them in a way that makes sense to do.

When it is realised that the self idea really is only imagination and that nothing will secure it, then the search to try to secure and fix starts to lessen and the requirement for any sort of balm or medicine to ease the suffering caused by that will disappear.

Then more and more there is just a visceral, immediate, open, available response to whatever the body is saying. Because there is less and less confused interpretation about 'what does this say about ME'. In this absence of personalisation there might be other possibilities that hadn't been considered before. There are infinite ways of meeting what the body or brain is asking for.

It is no wonder that medication is often used for a mental unrest that has nothing to do with the actual physical illness. In many ways this is a necessary response to the confusion. But as confusion lessens, there is just an obviousness to the body. It is no longer hidden by the belief 'the body is me'. Symptoms from the body no longer send us into a tailspin of imagined concepts - what this means about me, my future, my relationships etc.

So all we can do is treat any illnesses in whatever way it makes sense to, while at the same time exploring the nature of reality and self.

We have no idea what physical changes may happen as the idea of a separate self gets less but one thing for sure the absence of confusion about who we are makes it more and more clear what the body is.

## 19

## Diagnoses, labels and concepts

*This image of yourself is obviously not real.*
*Any more than the idea of a tree is a tree.*
*Any more than you can get wet in the word 'water'.*
**Alan Watts**

When it comes to a diagnosis, labels and concepts it can be very hard to see the distinction between imagination and reality.

And it can easily look like we are sliding into denial and spiritual bypass the moment we start talking about no objective reality.

Yet it is distinction between life lived in actual reality and the exhaustion of fighting the demons of imagination.

It can even be the difference between health and physically harmful events in the body as demonstrated by the nocebo effect.

Imagine sitting in a doctor's office, or maybe you

already have had this experience, and hearing a diagnosis. A one word label with explanation and prognosis.

What does that one word label do? Does it send the mind into a spiral of dread? Does it create a series of future scenarios each more terrible than the previous? Does it plunge the mind back into the past, scavenging for causes and regrets? Does it take on the minds and lives of the people we love - imagining the impact on them emotionally, physically, practically and mentally?

One word - and it creates a montage drawn from every film we've ever watched, everything seen on tv, what we've heard from friends, what we've googled, every headline. A hotchpotch of beliefs that create this unquestioned reality. And instantly there is a future rolling out that looks absolutely real. But it couldn't be less real. There is not one grain of truth in it.

The power of words and concepts on the mind, which we could say, is itself made of words and concepts, is immeasurable. And it has nothing to do with the reality.

Because nothing has changed. We are still sitting there, just as before, in the doctor's office. All that has changed is a hyper activity of mental imagining of self and other.

This chapter is an invitation to notice that a concept or a diagnosis eg. cancer or ADHD or autism or Cystic Fibrosis is only a frame for information.

For example, the word tomorrow contains possible information about tomorrow. It creates a space in which ideas can be discussed and information can be found out. It is a container of possibility.

It is not a description of now. It is not a description of actual reality. The places the mind goes when the word tomorrow is mentioned are pure imagination. The scenes that come to mind, the ideas of what will happen are creations of thought and belief. They are not true in any sense whatsoever.

That is sanity.

To understand the word tomorrow as simply a container of information is sanity. To understand any concept, including any diagnosis, any label, including any concept of 'me', 'you', 'them', 'future' and 'past' as a container of information is sanity.

Believing that the images that come to mind when the word tomorrow is mentioned have anything to do with reality is insane.

And yet we all do it.

Why?

Perhaps because the mind is so powerful, everything it conjures up looks real.

Perhaps because we have never been taught the distinction between now (reality) and not now (imagination).

Perhaps because the self identity itself is so powerfully believed and acts like a spider at the centre of the web.

Whatever the reason, the obviousness of reality / not reality is missed all the time.

This of course can create immense stress. It can create illness. It can exacerbate symptoms. It can even bring about an earlier death.

On a webinar one evening, we discussed how if all 40 of us brought to mind a picture of water, not one single one of those images would be anything other than imagination.

And this is why this spiritual understanding is entirely about the real world. It brings us out of that imagined space of a made up reality to just responding in the here and now to whatever is being said right now, to what could be useful right now.

The flights of fantasy and imagination are evidence of

the immensely creative mind, which is an enormous asset but it is not representing reality. It is the space of pure imagination.

Our system is designed to have that capacity of imagination.

Which is amazing. And wonderful. And an enormous gift of being human.

The problem comes when we try to solve the problems created by that imagination.

They cannot be solved. Because they are not real.

But it is so so hard to realise this.

Which is why we are so exhausted and desperate in the futile attempt to do so.

The response to actual reality on the other hand, the response to what is actually happening now, solving the issue that is real and right here now.

That we can do.

## 20

## Illness and acceptance

*In all the years I've practiced, which is over thirty years now, I've only rarely, if ever met anyone who really understood what their problem was. Because if we really know what the problem is, it evaporates, or a simple solution becomes obvious.*
**Roger Linden**

It is interesting to look at acceptance in relation to illness. There is a big deal made of acceptance and it seems a very spiritual thing. It looks like in that acceptance there will be freedom and peace.

So say we are ill. We might be feeling really awful. We might have all sorts of worries and concerns about the illness.

Then in comes a book or a teacher or well-meaning friend suggesting that, to find peace, we must accept the situation. So we try to do that. We try to accept the suffering. We try to accept our worst fears. We try to accept a reality that the whole body and mind is resisting.

But how can the mind, that creates that suffering in the first place, ever accept it? The mind is resistance. The idea that it has to accept what its entire activity is resisting is ridiculous. And so the attempt at acceptance sets up an exhausting mental battle - the never ending resistance of resistance.

Mental health is the understanding that the creations of the mind, the projections into the future, the concepts, the story of self have nothing to do with the actual physical sensations of right now. All the ideas, thoughts, projections are creations of imagination that look like reality.

This mental activity though looks like reality so it appears that this is the reality we have to accept.

The attempt to accept this reality will inevitably fail. Not least because there is nothing actually there to accept. Then of course there is self blame and despair because it looked as thought acceptance was the only way out.

So not only is there possibly some serious physical pain and discomfort there is also the mental chaos of these impossible attempts to accept the unacceptable.

So let's find some freedom in that because no one needs that chaos. Especially when we're ill.

How about we consider acceptance as being simply an 'openness to reality', a presence to what is actually happening now. Witnessing what is happening now is the closest we can get to reality. And even in that there is a great deal of 'unreal' but we can put the spotlight on that and see where the reality is.

Immersion in reality would only be the experience of physical sensation. Not even the labelling of it. Just the sensation itself. That's all. If we think of an illness, there is the feeling of it right now. There might be pain or aching, tension, discomfort. Anything might be happening now. A physical sensation right now. Acceptance is going deeply into that sensation.

For example, let's say we have a migraine. Acceptance would be to explore the reality of the pain. Not even exploring 'the migraine' as the label is always at least one step removed from the actual sensation. Going deeply into the reality of sensation and, at the same time, noticing the stories and projections that arise, that have nothing to do with the pain and nothing to do with reality.

As we go in and in and in to the pain, it changes beyond recognition. We are not doing this to get rid of the pain - that is just resistance - but to see the reality of it. That in-depth enquiry is acceptance. It is getting so close to it that it gives itself up to us. There is no separation between the explorer and the explored. There is just opening to whatever that physical sensation is.

That is reality. As close as we can get to it. The observation moves way beyond the label. Even the simple word 'pain' is heavily laden with association. We can't accept 'pain' as a concept, that is not real, it is a bundle of meaning and interpretation. But openness to, acceptance of the sensation is possible. Because that is reality.

We can distinguish between the actual momentary reality, the presence of sensation and every layer of unreality which is built around that sensation which is the mind going off on tangents with concepts, labels, fears and beliefs. None of that can ever be accepted because there is nothing there. There is nothing that doesn't squirm away and become something else.

When we come into the simple reality of what is happening right now, there is response to that. There is the honouring of that. No resistance. No thoughts of how this should be different. There is just this.

## WELL

That is the sanity of acceptance. Everything else is a mission impossible that only adds more exhaustion, confusion and resistance.

## 21

## Denial and intimacy

*Many spiritual people are involved in a radical denial of what is happening. They want to transcend it, get rid of it, get out of it, get away from it. There's nothing wrong with that feeling, but the approach doesn't work because it's escapism in spiritual clothing. It's wearing spiritual clothing and spiritual concepts, but it is really no different than a drunk in the gutter who doesn't want to feel the pain anymore. When you abide and accept everything completely and fully, you automatically go beyond.*
**Adyashanti**

I was at a non-duality retreat and asked a question about the brain.

'There is no brain' came the immediate reply. And, ultimately, we can't argue with that. This is true. There is no objective reality of the brain. Just as there is no objective reality of anything. An entire reality held in perception. No self. No other. No brain.

But if we have concussion or dizziness or constant headaches, to tell ourselves 'there is no brain' and equally 'there is no concussion or dizziness or headache' seems to be only a denial. A way of avoiding facing what is there to be faced. An apparently 'spiritual' way to turn the gaze from something that is actually calling to be considered more closely.

This is the ultimate challenge of our evolving spiritual understanding. Ensuring that a nascent revelation of the transient, subjective nature of all reality does not veer into denial whenever our idea of self or reality is challenged.

When current experience is pushed away with 'that isn't real' then all that is happening is spiritual bypass. Pain, anger, problems, shame and fears are squashed down, numbed and hidden away. Which ultimately, as we all know, only makes them find other ways to be acknowledged.

What do we do with this? How do we explore the transient nature of reality while not using it to escape that which is hard to face?

It seems there is only one way to know the difference between deep understanding and spiritual bypass and it is this:

*In true understanding, reality is revealed.*

That's it.

Deep understanding is the light of pure, open, presence, absent of judgement. It is the light of transformation. Realisation allows everything to be experienced, nothing to be pushed away. Pre-conceived ideas, beliefs, judgements, fears of self and other are met with love and in that love they give themselves up, never to return.

In that presence, there is nothing to deny because the reality no longer exists in the form it did before.

In that light, there is nothing to accept or detach from because there is only what is.

In that love, there is nothing even to forgive because no wrong exists.

This is not static. Authentic, dynamic behaviour comes from this presence. Appointments can be made, treatments and operations can be undergone, information can be sought, interventions can be practiced - all without any sense of separation. All without any confusion.

With spiritual bypass, on the other hand, there is no immersion in or presence to the apparent reality. It is just ignored or denied or covered over with empty concepts which only serves to make the reality more apparently concretely fixed.

'It's not real,' we say as we push away symptoms, or the terror of a diagnosis.

'It's just my thinking,' as we try to ignore the desperation of our anxiety.

'There is no self,' as we numb our shame or our needs and addictions.

And in being ignored and denied, these things clamour more and more loudly within our being.

We can say 'there is no brain' but until we have known the brain to such an extent that it gives itself up to us (and through us to all), it remains real, separate and distant. There is a brain.

We can say 'there is no other' but until we are with that other in such presence that the truth of who they are shines out through all the layers of separation, the other remains. There is another.

We can say 'there is no self' but until we sit with that self through the discomfort, through the defences, through the resistance, the shame, needs and fears, the self remains. Nothing has changed. There is a self.

To resume the rightful place of no-self, in order to melt back into the love, freedom and potential from which we arose, it is attention that is required not denial, openness not spiritual short cuts, presence not bypass.

## 22

## Pain

*You have tried everything, everything, except the obvious: accepting your pain, being present with it, today. Now, let's be clear about this: acceptance does not mean giving up on the possibility that the pain will lessen or even disappear tomorrow, or next week, or next year. It just means that your peace is no longer dependent on whether or not this happens.*
**Jeff Foster**

Often, a question comes up about physical pain. And of course the risk in a conversation about no objective reality is that the pain and the experience of the individual is dismissed as 'just your thinking' or even 'there is no body therefore there is no pain'.

And the teacher gets to look clever and the individual retreats shamefully back into their silent world of suffering, apparently not spiritual enough to live free from arthritis, migraines or sciatica.

So how do we walk this tightrope of the absolute realness (and imprisonment) of the individual experience and the understanding (and liberation) that there is no reality?

How do we do that without negating and denial? Without loading more suffering and self-blame into a mind that is already drowning in it?

A good place to start is in the body. In the raw sensations that sing out before words get to them, The body is as close to reality as it is possible to get. It is the intelligence of life in form and its every movement, message, indication and sensation is integral to the living system.

In its raw state, this information is critical, but neutral, feedback on the demands and requirements of the system.

It is real time reporting to which the whole system can seamlessly respond. That's the design. It's the deer shaking out the stress of the wolf attack. It's the roots of the plant moving away from a patch of toxic earth. It's our own liver and inner ear silently compensating for that bottle of red and our lungs and heart bringing equilibrium after the run for the bus.

An incredible, unfathomable system of life in form.

And what happens is that the information of this system, instead of being taken as what it is - information about the system - is labelled, bundled into concepts and transported into the illusory reality of the ever-active mind.

The sensations, instead of being sensations, now become evidence of whatever narrative of self is in place: failure or bleak futures or unfairness or whatever it is.

The entire raison d'être of pain is to draw attention to itself. Like a warning light on a car. It is drawing attention to that part of the system.

And is that all it is doing? I say 'all' without in any way meaning to dismiss the potential intensity and indeed torture of that experience.

I mean 'all' in the sense of - is it only information about the real time status of that specific area?

Or has the pain been packaged up by the mind and

transported into the far reaching lands: the future, the past, the reactions of others, the implications on jobs, the possible meaning behind the pain, the failure of the body.

If so, then the system is entirely disrupted. Because the signal of pain is designed to bring the attention into the body, into this moment, into reality. It is not designed to throw the mind into the exhaustive effort of trying instantly to solve imaginary problems, to pin down and predict the unpindownable and unpredictable.

So instead of the pain fulfilling its function, it is misunderstood. And every time it fires, the mind is transported into a reality than has nothing to do with the actuality of what is happening.

And because the pain is now evidence of the mind's worst fears, the mind is on high alert. Every twinge sends it off into the full force of its resistance, stress and anxiety.

In misunderstanding, the pain is ignored, other than as evidence of the narrative which is ruminated on, feasted on by the active mind.

In understanding, this is reversed. The pain, the signal, the essentially neutral indication of the system is all there is. It is honoured as a King would honour soldiers bringing information from impenetrable lands. And the narrative? That hotch potch of fears, shames and needs that has scooped up the pain and is using it as evidence of its veracity? That can be there, no problem. It has no meaning though, no truth, no information. And when that is seen, the compulsion to spend time in it ebbs away.

Pain can bring the attention back to reality, to the intelligence of a miracle system.

Or it does the opposite.

23

## Death

*Love, love, love, says Percy.*
*And hurry as fast as you can*
*along the shining beach, or the rubble, or the dust.*
*Then, go to sleep.*
*Give up your body heat, your beating heart.*
*Then, trust.*
**Mary Oliver**

Two quotes can help us sum up what we are looking at here.

The first is from Bill Bryson's exceptional book *'The Body, a guide for occupants'* in which he quotes the expert in trauma surgery, Ben Ollivere: 'Killing yourself is actually difficult. We are designed not to die'.

The second is the title of a book written by Richard Sylvester, named after the words that Tony Parsons once said to him, 'I hope you die soon'.

And hopefully it is clear, by this stage in this book, that the 'you' referred to in each quote is not the same 'you'.

'We are not designed to die' refers to the body, this

miracle of design, this 'universe of 37.2 trillion cells operating in more or less perfect concert' as Bill Bryson describes it.

The body is intelligence in action. And it is life that creates, of this lump of inert flesh and bone, a system of response and stasis that even the most eminent brains are still only beginning to fathom. All of it working, as far as it possibly can to maintain and prolong heath, vitality and function.

The self identity has no control or say in any of these physical processes. There is a belief that it does. But even just a moment's reflection shows that thought has no control over this most intricate, complex and unknown of systems. Indeed, the self idea is a product of the system, not the ruler of it.

Which is why we have the second quote, 'I hope you die soon'. Tony Parsons wasn't referring, of course, to the body. He was referring to that self identity that believes it is in charge, not just of the body but of everything - experience, emotion, beliefs, state…

Because it is that self identity that is the source of all suffering. The self identity is not necessary for life to flourish. The self identity is not necessary for this miracle system to function.

Indeed we could say that the protection of a self identity, the living out and defending of its insecurities and beliefs is the source of all violence, cruelty and conflict.

The self identity is a confusion of mind that the body often needs to work hard to flourish within. Think of the smoking habits and physical risks initiated to fit in. Think of the alcohol downed to numb shame or fears. Think of the drugs used to bolster self esteem and bravado. Think of the needless plastic surgery to look how we think we should look.

And sometimes, in the case of suicide for example, the body, try as it might—and it really will try—just cannot win the battle against the conviction that life as this self is not worth living.

The intelligence of this physical system is unquantifiable. The human capacity for imagination and conceptualisation, for ideas and thought is equally limitless.

And when the two are understood for what they are, when the idea of a controlling self dies in the face of the unknowable intelligence of life that we really are, then the life we are is lived with the freedom, respect and awe we deserve.

# 24

## Healing

*The very sense of being a person, the sense of being somewhat contracted and constricted is what creates that sense that 'I'm in prison'.*
**Richard Sylvester**


We could consider that all reality - of self, other, past, future, everything - is essentially a film. A film created from thought, belief, association and imagination.

And the immediate question (especially in a conversation about physical and mental health) might come 'Well that's all very well but I need to know how do I get into a new film? A film in which I am healthy/happy/strong/clear-minded/loved/admired/free? A film in which I am not depressed, anxious, lonely, trapped, ill or exhausted?'

In other words - how do I use this understanding to get a better experience?

It seems like the film analogy breaks down completely

because the thing about films - on the ipad, on the tv, even in the movies - is that they can be changed.

If we don't like the film then we can just tap a button and bingo a new film appears.

And in the cinema we can walk out. Find another screen.

Yet this film of our own lives can sometimes seem to be on continual repeat with no button to press, no green exit light showing our escape route.

What's happening there? If it's only a film, why can't it be changed?

Well it can be. Easily. But first we have to understand how these films work and in that understanding we can see where healing lies.

1. If the film is bad, it's because it's demanding to be seen for what it is

A film in which we are trapped, anxious, ill, depressed, contracted, limited or exhausted is a film so out of line with the infinite potential of life that its very existence is saying, 'there's something not quite true about this…'

2. The nature of the film (aka 'reality') must be understood

The film is a creation of self understanding. So everything that appears in 'reality', everything we resist or want to change is there because of the way the self is understood. Being on our own can be lonely or delicious. Having no money or no possessions or no home or no job can be our worst nightmare or a life-style choice. Pain can be something to fight against or the gift of information. Being terrified can be something to avoid at all costs or exhilarating. Being constrained or physically restricted can be something to struggle against or it can give rise to the greatest leaps of creativity.

It is the mind that makes it so. As John Milton said in

Paradise Lost, "The mind is its own place, and in itself can make a Heav'n of Hell, a Hell of Heav'n."

The belief in an insecure, limited self is always going to create suffering. Because it is not true. Yet it is from that misunderstanding that this film originates. And the suffering is the sign that it is time for a new film.

3. In the film, notice the uncomfortable

This is where the film starts to change. The uncomfortable is anything that threatens the idea of self. It is the story of the self that must be upheld, because, after all, what would we be without it? It is what must be defended or protected. And up until now, we've avoided the uncomfortable at all cost. We have turned away from it, squashed it down, numbed it, distracted ourselves from it, denied it, blocked it...

4. In the film, stay with or move towards the uncomfortable

Now we are going to do the opposite of avoidance or denial. We are going to hang out in the uncomfortable. The only thing at risk in doing this, is the self identity - which is just a collection of thoughts. So while exploring the nature of reality (step 2), we are also going to notice what makes us uncomfortable in the knowledge that this is the place of all change. We are going to move towards it, stay with that feeling. Explore it like an anthropologist would encounter a distant people. With curiosity, fascination. With nothing to lose but an old idea.

5. Change happens with the readiness to do the uncomfortable or to not do the comfortable

In our reality, there will be things that make the self uncomfortable. It will be anything that increases that feeling of vulnerability, of shame, fear and insecurity. It can be anything. Perhaps the prompt to join an exercise class or sport, ask for help, put ourselves out in the world or take up an activity or join a group. Whatever it is, it is an invitation to explore the protection of the self, to notice the increase in symptoms, to be the explorer in the terrain of what is outside the comfortable prison of the self identity.

Or there might be something that looks like it will make us more comfortable. In other words, there will be something that will create a distraction or numbing of the suffering of separation or a momentary 'reward' for the ego. It might be to lose ourself in the internet or sex or a bottle or the fridge. It might be to seek out approval or attention. Or to withdraw. Whatever it is, perhaps the inclination for this will fall away because there just isn't the desire any more to avoid the only genuinely useful information of our existence. Discovering who we really are might have become so much more interesting than comfort.

6. In the film, notice what then happens to the uncomfortable

What has just happened? We have challenged the self identity by moving into an area previously protected and defended. We have given up the comfort of the familiar story. Or moved towards the discomfort of the unknown.

And what might happen is that we now feel more vulnerable than ever. This is the ultimate self-check. Because the question is now: do we retreat back into the safety of the awful but comfortingly familiar film, or do we stay with the discomfort, notice it, move into it and continue to do what is uncomfortable to do in the knowledge that comfort cannot be found here? There is no respite for the identity.

7. Repeat steps 1-6

If we deeply question what is true and if we stay with, move into and do the uncomfortable or don't do the comfortable, we move into a whole new understanding of self and reality. A self with less and less layers of protection. A reality which is more and more aligned to the freedom, peace, love and potential of our true nature.

A new film is playing, and then another new film. And then another. Until the film that is playing is the perfect expression of our existence.

And, at that point, it becomes clear.

There was never anything to change.

# PART V

# Conclusion

*You believe that you live in the
universe when in reality the universe lives in you.*
**Steve Chandler**

# 25

## Conclusion

*If you desire healing,*
*let yourself fall ill*
*let yourself fall ill.*
**Rumi**

At the moment of writing this chapter, the on-line course 'WELL: getting real with mental and physical health' is underway. I have had emails this morning from four different people on the course all saying essentially the same thing:

'Make the suffering stop. It is overwhelming. Take away the anguish. Make me feel better. I've tried everything. This is my last hope.'

Maybe we all know that desperation. It might not be suffering in relation to health. It might be about our partner or money or family or career or anything.

But the plea is the same 'make the suffering stop'. And we try everything to get rid of it. All the time trying to get rid of the sensation of dis-ease, discomfort, insecurity, desperation through whatever means available.

And all the focus and effort is on the pushing away and numbing, on the resisting and squashing.

There is no enquiry into what is actually causing the suffering. And I don't mean what is causing the pain or the illness - I mean what is causing the resistance to whatever is, the idea that what is should be different.

None of the attention is on what is actually true. The cacophony of thoughts about the future, the past, the comparisons with others, the identity that springs from the suffering goes unquestioned.

There is pushing away of whatever is being experienced and there is complete belief in whatever is being thought.

And that is the way of it.

That is the conditioned sleepwalking that we are all doing until a kiss from a prince (or perhaps a book... if indeed books can kiss... I'm sure they can... ) breaks the trance and wakes us up.

And the waking state is reality. It is sanity and truthfulness and just what is.

The waking is the opposite of the sleepwalking.

In sleepwalking, we resist experience, we resist the sensations of the body and live the unquestioned reality of thought and belief.

The waking state turns that upside down. The body, that fluid living intelligence, is honoured, noticed, attended to. The narrative story is understood for what it is - the workings of a frantic mind.

The waking is simply presence to all of this.

The waking is the realisation that no thought or belief or concept, including that epicentre of the whole caboodle - the concept of self, is true.

# WELL

There is no peace or freedom for the thought-created self no matter how hard it tries to control itself and the world around it.

The peace and freedom are there already. It's just that all that searching for them is obscuring them.

The revelation of that peace and freedom is what we had been looking for all along. And the search had made us iller, more burdened and more exhausted.

Now there is the falling away of what we are not. The ending of the search for the unobtainable.

The simple sanity of living as the pure source intelligence that we are.

In every sense… well.

## About the Author

Clare Dimond runs live and on-line programmes exploring how excellence, freedom, love and creativity are our natural state.

For materials, resources, programmes or to ask any questions raised by this book, visit www.claredimond.com

## Also by Clare Dimond

GAME: Getting real with the play of life

REAL: The inside-out guide to being yourself

FREE: The inside-out guide to life unlimited

EASE: The inside-out guide to getting real with work

SANE: Getting real with reality

Printed in Great Britain
by Amazon